W9-AKC-593

Free-Range Chickens

ALSO BY SIMON RICH

Ant Farm

Free-Range
Chickens

Simon Rich

RANDOM HOUSE

NEW YORK

LINDENHURST MEMORIAL LIBRARY
LINDENHURST, NEW YORK 11757

Copyright © 2008 by Simon Rich

All rights reserved.

Published in the United States by Random House, an imprint of
The Random House Publishing Group, a division
of Random House, Inc., New York.

RANDOM HOUSE and colophon are registered trademarks
of Random House, Inc.

"What I Imagined People Around Me Were Saying"
was originally published as "Hey, Look" in *The New Yorker,* July 23, 2007.
"Actor's Nightmare," "Amusement," and "Free-Range Chickens" were
originally published, in different form, in *The Harvard Lampoon.*

LIBRARY OF CONGRESS CATALOGING-IN-PUBLICATION DATA
Rich, Simon.
Free-range chickens / Simon Rich.
p. cm.
ISBN 978-1-4000-6589-9
I. American wit and humor.   I. Title.
PN6165.R54 2008
818'.602—dc22   2008003036

Printed in the United States of America on acid-free paper

www.atrandom.com

2 4 6 8 9 7 5 3 1

FIRST EDITION

Book design by Simon M. Sullivan

FOR DAD AND ALEX

Contents

II

GOING TO WORK

III

DAILY LIFE

IV

RELATIONSHIPS

V

ANIMALS

VI

GOD

author's note

This is a joke book that I wrote. Nothing in it is real.
It's just some things that I made up.

I

GROWING UP

Terrifying childhood experiences

—Got your nose!
—Please just kill me. Better to die than to live the rest of my life as a monster.

—What's that in your ear? Hey—it's a quarter!
—Why is everybody laughing? I have a horrifying brain disease.

—Peek-a-boo!
—Jesus Christ. You came out of nowhere.

When I lost my first tooth

ME: You're never going to believe this. I was hanging out with my friends and all of a sudden, a tooth fell out of my mouth. I think there's something seriously wrong with me.

MOM: Looks like the tooth fairy's coming to town!

ME: Who?

MOM: The tooth fairy. She visits children in the middle of the night and takes their teeth.

ME: Is she . . . a cannibal?

MOM: No, she's a fairy.

ME: What else does she take? Does she take *eyes*?

MOM: No, just teeth. And when she's done, she leaves a surprise under your pillow.

ME: Oh my God.

MOM: I wonder what it'll be this time?

ME: Okay . . . let's not panic here. There's got to be a way to trap her or kill her. We just need to *think*.

MOM: You don't want to kill the tooth fairy.

ME: Why not? Wait a minute . . . I see what's going on. You're in *cahoots* with her! God, it all makes sense now . . . how else would she know that I had lost a tooth in the first place?

MOM: I think someone's getting a little sleepy.

ME: Wait until Dad finds out about this!

MOM: He knows about the tooth fairy, sweetie.

ME: Jesus Christ. How high up does this thing go?

MOM: Let's get you tucked in.

ME: Listen . . . as long as we're laying it all on the line, you might as well be straight with me. What other fairies are you working with? Is there a *face* fairy?

MOM: There's just a tooth fairy, sweetie. She comes every time you lose a tooth.

ME: What do you mean "every time"? I'm going to lose more teeth?

MOM: You're going to lose all of them.

A conversation between the people who hid in my closet every night when I was seven

FREDDY KRUEGER: When do you guys want to kill him?

MURDERER FROM THE SIX O'CLOCK NEWS: How about right now?

DEAD UNCLE WHOSE BODY I SAW AT AN OPEN CASKET FUNERAL: I say we do it when he gets up to pee. You know, when he's walking down the hallway, in the dark.

FREDDY KRUEGER: What if he doesn't get up?

MURDERER: He'll get up. Look at how he's squirming. It's only a matter of time.

DEAD UNCLE: Man, I cannot *wait* to kill this kid.

MURDERER: Same here.

FREDDY KRUEGER: I've wanted to kill him ever since he saw my movie.

DEAD UNCLE: Hey, do you guys remember that night-light Simon used to have?

MURDERER: Man, that thing scared the heck out of me.

FREDDY KRUEGER: It's a good thing his mom got rid of it. Now there's nothing to stop us from killing him.

(Everyone nods in agreement.)

DR. MURPHY: Hey, guys, sorry I'm late. I was busy scheduling an appointment with Simon, to give him shots.

FREDDY KRUEGER: No problem.

(Freddy Krueger and Dr. Murphy do their secret handshake.)

MURDERER: It's getting kind of crowded in here. Chucky, can you move over?

CHUCKY: I'm over as far as I can get.

MURDERER: I need more space than you're giving me. I'm a lot bigger than you.

CHUCKY: Are you calling me *short?*

DR. MURPHY: Hey, guys, *relax,* all right? We're all here for the same reason: to kill and possibly eat Simon.

MURDERER: *(Sighs.)* You're right. I'm sorry.

CHUCKY: Yeah . . . me too. I kind of lost perspective.

DR. MURPHY: It's okay. Just remember: we're all in this together.

DEAD UNCLE: Hey, it looks like he's getting up! Wait a minute . . . where's he *going?*

CHUCKY: I think he's running into his mom's room!

DEAD UNCLE: Maybe we should follow him?

CHUCKY: Are you *insane?* I'm not facing that kid's mother. That woman is terrifying!

MURDERER: Seriously, there is no *way* I'm going in there.

FREDDY KRUEGER: *(Sighs.)* I guess tonight's a bust. Let's try tomorrow, okay? Same time, same place.

If adults were subjected to the same indignities as children

PARTY

ZOE: Dad, I'm throwing a party tonight, so you'll have to stay in your room. Don't worry, though: one of my friends brought over his father for you to play with. His name is Comptroller Brooks and he's about your age, so I'm sure you'll have lots in common. I'll come check on you in a couple of hours. *(Leaves.)*

COMPTROLLER BROOKS: Hello.

MR. HIGGINS: Hello.

COMPTROLLER BROOKS: So . . . um . . . do you follow city politics?

MR. HIGGINS: Not really.

COMPTROLLER BROOKS: Oh.

(long pause)

(Zoe returns.)

ZOE: I forgot to tell you: I told my friends you'd perform for them after dinner. I'll come get you when it's time. *(Leaves.)*

COMPTROLLER BROOKS: Oh God, what are we going to *do*?

MR. HIGGINS: I know a dance . . . but it's pretty humiliating.

COMPTROLLER BROOKS: Just teach it to me.

CAPITOL HILL

LOBBYIST: If you fail to pass this proposition, it will lead to the deaths of thousands. Any questions?

SENATOR: Why are you wearing a sailor suit?

LOBBYIST: My children decided to dress me this way, on a whim. I told them it was an important day for me . . . but they wouldn't listen.

SENATOR: It's adorable.

LOBBYIST: Okay . . . but . . . do you agree with the proposition? About the war?

SENATOR: Put on the cap.

GARAGE

ALBERT ROSENBLATT: Can I drive your car? I'll give it back when I'm done.

MRS. HERSON: I'm sorry . . . do I know you?

ALBERT ROSENBLATT: No, but we're the same age and we go to the same garage.

MRS. HERSON: No offense, sir, but I really don't feel comfortable lending you my car. I mean, it's by far my most important possession.

PARKING ATTENDANT: Mrs. Herson! I'm *surprised* at you. What did we learn about sharing?

MRS. HERSON: You're right . . . I'm sorry. Take my Mercedes.

ALBERT ROSENBLATT: Thank you. Can I come over to your house later? I'm lonely and I don't have any friends.

MRS. HERSON: Well . . . actually . . . I kind of had plans tonight.

PARKING ATTENDANT: Are you *excluding* him?

MRS. HERSON: No, of course not! *(Sighs.)* Here's my address, sir. The party starts at eight.

ALBERT ROSENBLATT: I'll show up a little early.

MRS. HERSON: What's that on your face?

ALBERT ROSENBLATT: Mucus. I haven't learned how to blow my nose yet, so I just go around like this all the time.

MRS. HERSON: Oh.

ALBERT ROSENBLATT: I'll see you soon, inside of your house.

My top secret seventh-grade diary

TUESDAY

Beware! If ye hath stumbled upon this secret tome, ye must put it downeth immediately! Thine eyes are not meant to readeth these words! Indeed, if thy continue to readeth, a most horrible curse shall fall upon your very soul!

Today I went to school. Afterwards I watched Charles in Charge and Murphy Brown.

WEDNESDAY

Beware! He who readeth this scripture will surely come to a horrible end, for these precious words exist for mine eyes— and mine eyes alone!

Went to school, came home, watched Charles in Charge, Murphy Brown and The Hogan Family.

THURSDAY

O heavenly beasts, with horns of iron and wings of steel, I summon you to earth to unleash your wicked torments upon they who dare to readeth these words! Curse them! Curse them a thousand times over! For to read this consecrated tome is to rip open mine heart and feast upon its sacred truths!

Charles in Charge, Murphy Brown, The Hogan Family, Three's Company, Murphy Brown rerun, The Hogan Family.

FRIDAY

Oh my God, I just found out they're canceling The Hogan Family. I don't know what to do. My fingers are shaking so much it's hard to hold the pencil. I've been crying for three straight hours and I can't make myself stop. There's a chance they might show reruns in the summer but I'm not even sure if they'll do that. I've never felt so lonely and scared in my entire life. My Mom's going to get home from work soon and I'm going to have to go out there and smile and somehow pretend like everything's all right. But on the inside I'll be screaming at the top of my lungs, screaming with anger and fear. It's times like this that I wonder if you even exist, God. Where were you today? Just hanging out? Well, guess what? The Hogan Family was *canceled*. The third best show of the year, gone forever. Like so much dust in the wind.

SATURDAY

Who's the Boss marathon.

Frogs

—Hey, can I ask you something? Why do human children dissect us?

—It's part of their education. They cut open our bodies in school and write reports about their findings.

—Huh. Well, I guess it could be worse, right? I mean, at least we're not dying in vain.

—How do you figure?

—Well . . . our deaths are furthering the spread of knowledge. It's a huge sacrifice we're making, but at least some good comes out of it.

—Let me show you something.

—What's this?

—It's a frog dissection report.

—Who wrote it?

—A fourteen-year-old human from New York City. Some kid named Simon.

— *(flipping through it)* This is it? This is the whole thing?

—Uh-huh.

—Geez . . . it doesn't look like he put a whole lot of time into this.

—Look at the diagram on the last page.

—Oh my God . . . it's so *crude*. It's almost as if he wasn't even looking down at the paper while he was drawing it. Like he was watching *TV* or something.

—Read the conclusion.

—*In conclusion, frogs are a scientific wonder of biology.* What does that even mean?

—It doesn't mean anything.

—Why are the margins so big?

—He was trying to make it look as if he had written five pages, even though he had only written four.

—He couldn't come up with one more page of observations about our dead bodies?

—I guess not.

—This paragraph looks like it was copied straight out of an encyclopedia. I'd be shocked if he retained any of this information.

—Did you see that he spelled "science" wrong in the heading?

—Whoa . . . I missed that. That's incredible.

—He didn't even bother to run it through spell check.

—Who did he dissect?

—Harold.

—Betsy's husband? Jesus. So this is why Harold was killed. To produce this . . . "report."

— *(Nods.)* This is why his life was taken from him.

(long pause)

—Well, at least it has a cover sheet.

—Yeah. The plastic's a nice touch.

Middle-school
telephone conversation

—Jake, it's Simon, I have to tell you something!

—Wait, hold on—I have to tell *you* something.

—Trust me. My news is bigger.

—Oh yeah? I just won *fifty-two million dollars* in a Publishers Clearing House Sweepstakes that I don't even remember entering. How's that for big?

—Dude . . . I got the same letter.

—Are you sure? Did it have an official red ribbon on the front?

—Yeah.

—And a congratulatory autograph from Ed McMahon on the back?

—Uh-huh.

—Dude . . . do you realize what's going on here?

—No, what?

—Between the two of us, we have over *a hundred million dollars.*

—Oh my God . . . what are the odds?

—I can't even guess. Huge.

—Do you think anyone else in the class won?

—No way. Two is weird, but three would be crazy.

—Have you told anyone else besides me?

—I sent an e-mail to the class, telling them the news and cursing everybody out. I figure no one can touch me now.

—Wow. Do you have any idea what you're going to spend it on?

—I've already offered Mr. Allen twenty thousand to shave his mustache.

—What do you have against his mustache?

—Nothing. It's just a power thing.

—Has he written back?

—He will.

—Hey . . . now that we have this money . . . do you think Jessica will invite us to her Halloween party?

—Maybe. If we pay her, like, forty thousand dollars.

—Do you think it's worth it?

—Nah. What's so great about a stupid party? For that amount of money, we could buy eighty thousand Laffy Taffys.

—What would we do with all that candy?

—Swim in it. Buy a pool and *swim* in it.

—I'm glad you won, man. It would've been weird if it was just me.

—Same here, buddy.

Bar mitzvah

*After you have your bar mitzvah, you will be
a man in the eyes of God.*

—my rabbi

GOD: Any bar mitzvahs today?

ANGEL: Yes . . . Simon Rich has prepared twelve lines of Torah
for his congregation at Central Synagogue.

GOD: Ah, then he must be *very* manly!

ANGEL: *(hesitating)* Yes.

GOD: Has this man started a family?

ANGEL: Um . . . not yet.

GOD: I assume, though, that he has prospects?

ANGEL: I'm not sure I know how to answer that question.

GOD: I'd like to have a look at this strapping fellow! Where is
he?

ANGEL: In his bedroom. *(Points.)*

GOD: Oh. Well . . . I must admit he's not as robust as I would
have imagined, given his mastery of Torah. But appearances

aren't everything! He's having a bar mitzvah, and in my eyes, that makes him a man. What's that he's doing?

ANGEL: I believe he's playing a video game, sir. *Shufflepuck.*

GOD: Does it . . . have to do with Torah?

ANGEL: Well, actually, it's sort of like air hockey. Except . . . you play against space aliens, on a computer.

GOD: Why is he dancing?

ANGEL: I believe he just beat a challenging level.

GOD: So this dance is a kind of . . . celebration.

ANGEL: Yes.

GOD: I take it from his enthusiasm that this is the first time he's beaten this particular level.

ANGEL: Well, actually, he does this dance whenever he beats *any* level of *any* video game. See . . . there. He's doing it again.

GOD: Yes, I see. It's the same dance, all right.

ANGEL: It's usually not as . . . frenetic . . . as this. He's probably nervous about his upcoming bar mitzvah.

GOD: Who is that man, on the poster above his bed?

ANGEL: His name is Weird Al Yankovic.

GOD: I've never heard of him. Is he . . . a Talmudic scholar?

ANGEL: Um . . . yes.

Inside the cartridge: *Duck Hunt*

SCENE: GRASS PATCH RD.

—Thank God. The barrage is finally over.

—How many have perished?

— . . .

—Please, father. I'm old enough to know the truth.

—Thirty-six, son. Thirty-six of our fellow ducks . . . with thirty-six bullets.

—I don't understand. How could the killer have such perfect accuracy?

—Simple. He holds the gun so close to our bodies that it's physically impossible for him to miss us.

—But where's the sport in that?

—It isn't the challenge of the hunt that drives him, son. It's his sick thirst for blood.

—Jesus.

—There's more. It is said that the killer . . . is a child.

—Impossible.

—I'm just repeating what the elders have said.

—How could a child possibly have so much rage?

—I don't know. He clearly has emotional problems.

—How could his parents allow him to attack us like this, for so many hours a day and so many days in a row?

—They are blind.

—Good Lord . . . I think I hear something!

—It's starting up again.

—I hope he chooses to shoot clay discs this time.

—Hope is a dangerous thing, son.

Deal with God

When I was nine years old, I made the following prayer to God:

Dear Lord, if you save the sitcom *Perfect Strangers* from being canceled, I promise I'll start believing in you and going to synagogue every week.

Three weeks later, ABC announced that they were picking up *Perfect Strangers* for another thirteen episodes. And yet, despite this miracle, I continued to doubt God's existence.

GOD, PRESENT DAY

ANGEL: Quite a turnout in synagogue today! Look . . . the entire Rubinstein family showed up!
GOD: Stop trying to distract me. Did Simon come or not?
ANGEL: The service just started . . . maybe he'll come later?
GOD: Do you know how many strings I had to pull to get *Perfect Strangers* back on the air? It was unbelievably difficult.
ANGEL: I know, sir.

GOD: I had to kill ABC's head of programming and replace him with someone who liked the show.

ANGEL: I remember.

GOD: Do you know how many people prayed for me to *cancel* that show? Like four hundred people.

ANGEL: Maybe Simon would come to synagogue if you gave him another miracle?

GOD: Like what?

ANGEL: Well . . . he just sent you this prayer.

GOD: *(reading)* "Dear God, please fix this damn wireless Internet connection."

ANGEL: What do you think?

GOD: Well . . . the only way I can think of to fix his wireless connection is to strike all the power lines with lightning. And that could result in countless deaths.

ANGEL: I don't know if it's worth it, sir. Maybe we should just move on?

GOD: *(Shakes head.)* This is too important.

What I imagined the people around me were saying when I was . . .

ELEVEN

—Oh, man, I can't believe that kid Simon missed that ground ball! How pathetic!

—Wait . . . he's staring at his baseball glove with a confused expression on his face. Maybe there's something wrong with his glove and *that's* why he messed up?

—Yes, that's probably what happened.

TWELVE

—Did that kid sitting behind us on the bus just get an erection?

—I don't know. For a while, I thought that was the case, but now that he's holding a book on his lap, it's impossible to tell.

—I guess we'll never know what the situation was.

THIRTEEN

—Hey, look, that thirteen-year-old is walking around with his mom!

—Where?

—There—in front of the supermarket!

—Oh my God! That kid is *way* too old to be hanging out with his mom. Even though I've never met him, I can tell he's a complete loser.

—Wait a minute . . . he's scowling at her and rolling his eyes.

—Oh, yeah . . . and I think I just heard him curse at her, for no reason.

—I guess he's cool after all.

FOURTEEN

—Why does that kid have a black X on the back of his right hand?

—I bet it's because he went to some kind of cool rock concert last night.

—Wow . . . he must've stayed out pretty late if he didn't have time to scrub it off.

—Yeah, and that's probably why his hair is so messy and un-washed. Because he cares more about rocking out than con-forming to society.

—Even though he isn't popular in the traditional sense, I re-spect him from afar.

FIFTEEN

—Hey, look, that kid is reading *Howl* by Allen Ginsberg.

—Wow. He must be some kind of rebel genius.

—I'm impressed by the fact that he isn't trying to call attention to himself.

—Yeah, he's just sitting silently in the corner, flipping the pages and nodding, with total comprehension.

—It's amazing: he's so absorbed in his book that he isn't even aware that a party is going on around him, with dancing and fun.

—Why aren't any girls going over and talking to him?

—I guess they're probably a little intimidated by his brilliance.

—Well, who *wouldn't* be?

—I'm sure the girls will talk to him soon.

—It's only a matter of time.

SIXTEEN

—Hey, look, it's that kid Simon who wrote that scathing poem for the literary magazine.

—You mean the one about how people are phonies? Wow— I loved that poem!

—Me too. Reading it made me realize for the first time that everyone is a phony, including me.

—The only person at this school who isn't a phony is Simon.

—Yeah. He sees right through us.

How my mother imagined the police

FIRST OFFICER: I just got a call from a local mother. Apparently her child was supposed to be home by six—and he still hasn't arrived.

SECOND OFFICER: Jesus Christ. It's almost *seven*. Are you sure she told him to be home by six?

FIRST OFFICER: Yes, that's his weekday curfew: six P.M. If he stays out past that hour, he's supposed to call and tell her where he is.

SECOND OFFICER: And you're telling me he *still hasn't called*?

FIRST OFFICER: I know . . . it's a pretty scary situation.

SECOND OFFICER: We better get the chief.

CHIEF: Let me get this straight . . . the mother still hasn't received a call from her son?

FIRST OFFICER: No, Chief.

CHIEF: Then we can only assume the worst has happened.

SECOND OFFICER: You mean . . . a hit-and-run?

CHIEF: Either that or a kidnapping. They're both very real

possibilities. Get Washington on the horn. This is a job for the FBI.

FBI AGENT: All right, everybody, listen up. We've got a *Code Red.* A fifteen-year-old child has been missing for nearly an *hour* and he has had no contact whatsoever with his mother. Grab your guns and your helicopters and let's get moving!

FIRST OFFICER: *(shaking his head)* What's the point, sir? It's been so long . . . he's almost certainly dead!

FBI AGENT: *(Slaps him.)* We got to keep looking, for the mother's sake. Even if it's just to find the body.

SECOND OFFICER: *(in tears)* Chief, we found him! He was at a friend's house playing video games!

CHIEF: Oh, thank God—I thought for sure we'd lost him!

FBI AGENT: *(lighting a cigarette)* We got lucky this time. Let's hope to Christ there ain't a next time.

CHIEF: *(mopping the sweat off his face)* I'm getting too old for this.

FBI AGENT: All I can say is: Thank God that boy's mother called. If we hadn't located him when we did, he almost certainly would have been killed somehow.

Ninth-grade experiments

OBSERVATION: None of the girls in my class think that I'm cool.

RESEARCH: My older brother told me that the political hardcore band Rage Against the Machine is cool.

HYPOTHESIS: If I pretend to be really into the political hardcore band Rage Against the Machine, then the girls in my class will think that I'm cool.

MATERIALS:
    1 Rage Against the Machine album
    1 Rage Against the Machine T-shirt
    1 Rage Against the Machine bandanna

METHODS:
    1) Wear the T-shirt and bandanna every single day for an entire month.
    2) Make fun of everybody in the class for listening to bands that are less politically intense than Rage Against

the Machine. Especially make fun of the girls who I am trying to impress.

3) Quote Rage Against the Machine lyrics constantly, regardless of the situation.

4) If someone asks me what I'm talking about, roll my eyes and say, "You probably wouldn't get it. It has to do with communism."

5) If someone calls my bluff and asks me what communism is, bang my fist against the table and say, "*God, stop being such a poser!*"

WAS YOUR HYPOTHESIS CORRECT? No.

2

OBSERVATION: None of the girls in my class think that I'm cool.

RESEARCH: Mike Cobalt wears gel in his hair and the girls think he's cool.

HYPOTHESIS: If I wear gel in my hair, then the girls will think I'm cool.

MATERIAL:
1 large bottle of Dep Shaping Gel (Extra Super Hold)

METHODS:

1) Wear gel in my hair every day for a week.

2) When my mom stops me at the elevator every morning and begs to help me use the gel because I "don't understand how it works," become so furious with her that I'm almost at the brink of tears.

WAS YOUR HYPOTHESIS CORRECT? No.

· 3

OBSERVATION: None of the girls in my class think that I'm cool. But one of the girls in my history class has started being nice to me.

RESEARCH: Sometimes when I'm eating lunch alone in the cafeteria, she sits down next to me, voluntarily. One time, when the two of us were alone in an elevator, she said, "God, Saturdays are so boring. I wish someone would take me to a *movie* or something."

HYPOTHESIS: If I ask her out, she might say yes—as long as I do it in a super-slick way.

MATERIALS:
3 cans of Jolt cola

METHODS:

1) Go to the bathroom at lunch and drink all three cans of Jolt to "get pumped."
2) Walk around her table in a circle until she motions for me to sit down next to her.
3) Pretend that I just noticed for the first time that she was sitting in the cafeteria, even though it's basically empty except for me and her.
4) Sit down across from her.
5) When she asks me if everything is okay, because parts of my face are twitching, tell her that I'm fine.
6) Don't say anything for ten whole minutes.
7) Tell her that *The Waterboy* starring Adam Sandler is opening on Friday.
8) Wait a little while for that information to sink in.
9) When she asks me if I'm planning on seeing it, say yes.
10) When she asks me if I'm going to see it *with* anyone, say no.
11) Stare at my tray for a few minutes, until she pokes me on the shoulder and says, "Hey . . . do you want to ask *me* to go with you?"
12) Look up and nod.

WAS YOUR HYPOTHESIS CORRECT? Yes!

II

GOING TO WORK

Choose your own adventure

In Choose Your Own Adventure 17 you were a prince of England, *jousting your way to the throne! In Choose Your Own Adventure 46 you were a* boy rock star, *jamming your way up the charts! Now, in Choose Your Own Adventure 92, you're a* grown-up, *working as a Corporate Software Designer in Poughkeepsie.*

PAGE ONE

You wake up at 7:45. The alarm clock never went off, but it doesn't matter. You've gotten so used to waking up every single day at the same time that it just happens automatically now. You feel so horrible you can barely even believe it. Suddenly you remember that it's Wednesday. That means there's going to be one of those Projects Meetings and you're going to have to sit through the entire three-hour nightmare as soon as you get to work. Maybe you should just call in sick? You have three sick days and you've only used one so far. Then again, if you use your second sick day now, you'll only have one left.

If you decide to use your sick day now, turn to Page Two.
If you decide to save your sick day for some other time, turn to Page Six.

PAGE TWO

You call the office and tell them you're sick.

"That's your second sick day," Nancy tells you. "You only have one left."

"I know," you say, hanging up the phone.

How did this happen? How did this become your life?

You try to go back to sleep, but it's impossible. After about five minutes, you sit up and turn on the television. That's when you remember: the cable in your apartment is broken and the guy isn't coming to fix it until Saturday. You flip around for a while, but the only channels you get are CBS and NBC. CBS is playing *The Early Show.* NBC is playing the *Today* show.

If you decide to watch The Early Show *on CBS, turn to Page Three.*

If you decide to watch the Today *show on NBC, turn to Page Four.*

PAGE THREE

You watch *The Early Show.*

Turn to Page Five.

PAGE FOUR

You watch the *Today* show.

Turn to Page Five.

PAGE FIVE

You go to the bathroom and look at your face. What happened? You used to be young and it wasn't so long ago. Jesus. Maybe you should have just gone to work.

THE END

PAGE SIX

You go to work. The Projects Meeting is about as horrible as you expected. It's just the same thing every time. Mr. Cohen talking about "viability," and everybody nodding and looking at the clock, waiting for lunch to start, like a bunch of animals. When you get down to it, everybody is basically just an animal—eating, sleeping, eating, sleeping. Dying. Christ. Maybe you should have just called in sick.

THE END

Actor's nightmare

FORD'S THEATER, 1865

*(*LADY HAMPTON *and* LORD HAMPTON *enter stage right.)*

LADY HAMPTON: Good afternoon, sir.

LORD HAMPTON: Good afternoon.

(President Lincoln shot in the head.)

STAGE MANAGER: *(offstage)* Keep going!

Demands

Dear cops,

I'll release the hostages if you bring me the following items:

1) Combination to bank vault or some kind of machine that can open vaults
2) A strong bag that is big enough to fit all of the money from the vault
3) A second criminal to help me carry this bag out of the bank
4) Ropes to tie up the hostages so they don't walk around so much
5) A third criminal with a car who can drive us away as soon as we get outside with the bag
6) MapQuest directions from the bank parking lot to Mexico
7) Some general information on Mexico (what kind of currency they use, which sports are popular there, basic culture things)
8) English to Spanish dictionary
9) Someone needs to go back to my apartment and bring

me my asthma inhaler. It's either in the medicine cabinet or on the little table next to the futon.

10) There's a small chance I left the stove on in my apartment. I don't think I did, but I'm a little bit worried
because I can't actually visualize myself turning it off.
Anyway, whichever policeman goes to get the inhaler
should also check to make sure the burner is all the
way off because I left my cat behind and I don't want
him to inhale any gas.

11) I just realized that someone is going to have to adopt
my cat. His name is Rudy and he is very smart and af-
fectionate. I'm not just saying that because he is
mine—he is a really special animal. He has a slight
bladder problem but it's not bad as long as you give
him his medication (the directions are on the bottle).

12) I forgot to give Rudy his pill this morning. Just give
him two tonight. You're really not supposed to do it
like that, but it's okay if it ends up happening once in a
while.

13) Some kind of weapon.

Gotham City Hall

BATMAN: Thanks for taking the time to meet with me, Mayor.

MAYOR: Of course, Batman. What's on your mind?

BATMAN: It's about the prison system. I really think you should increase funding.

MAYOR: We've already been over this, Batman. We simply don't have the resources.

BATMAN: But Gotham City *needs* a maximum security prison. I mean . . . look at these statistics. *(Takes out pie chart.)* Scare-crow has escaped eleven times. The Riddler has escaped sixty-four times. The Joker has escaped *four thousand* times. It's like, what's the point of even *having* a prison?

MAYOR: I wish there was something I could do, but the annual budget's already been finalized.

BATMAN: You know these guys are trying to kill me, right?

MAYOR: I'll tell you what: I can transfer the Joker to the Asylum for the Criminally Insane. That's a secure location.

BATMAN: Are you kidding me? That place is a freaking *joke*!

MAYOR: . . .

BATMAN: I'm sorry . . . I was out of line.

MAYOR: That's all right. I know this is an emotional issue for you.

BATMAN: I just don't have any confidence in that asylum. Last month they released the Penguin and *three days later* he tried to kill me. I was able to capture him and have him recommitted to the asylum, but they released him again the very next day! He tried to kill me this morning. I barely escaped. He's still on the loose.

MAYOR: Believe me, Batman, I sympathize.

BATMAN: Listen. I've been crunching the numbers, and if we eliminate the Gotham Symphony Orchestra, we can hire four extra guards and build a watchtower.

MAYOR: Batman, the orchestra is one of the jewels of our city.

BATMAN: I know, I know . . . but don't you think we've reached a crisis situation?

MAYOR: It's just . . . less costly to keep things the way they are. And besides, you can handle these guys! You're *Batman*. You don't need some fancy, expensive new prison.

BATMAN: Is that new? That flat screen TV?

MAYOR: . . .

(Phone rings.)

MAYOR: Excuse me, Batman. *(Picks up phone.)* Mayor Hayes here . . . really? Kidnapped? What did the note say? Huh . . . it sounds like some kind of *riddle*. Nah, don't worry about the signal. He's right here. *(Hangs up.)* It seems the governor's daughter has been kidnapped.

BATMAN: Again? That's the third time this month!

MAYOR: It sounds like the work of the Riddler. Apparently he's . . . um . . . escaped from prison.

BATMAN: . . .

MAYOR: Hey, at least you're already dressed, right? I mean, that saves us a call on the red phone.

BATMAN: You know what my red phone bill was last month? Eleven hundred dollars. That money comes straight out of my own pocket.

MAYOR: Do you want a key to the city?

BATMAN: I already have seventy-four keys to the city. I don't need another key to the damn city. All I want is some accountability here.

MAYOR: I'll tell you what: I'll talk to that philanthropist, Bruce Wayne. I bet I can convince him to donate us a prison. That guy's a real pushover.

BATMAN: . . .

MAYOR: You know there's a rumor going around that he had a face-lift?

BATMAN: Really? Who's been saying that?

MAYOR: *(Shrugs.)* Everybody.

World's oldest profession

If prostitution really is the "world's oldest profession," that means there was a time when it was the only job on earth.

20,000 B.C.

MAN: Hey.

WOMAN: Hey.

MAN AND WOMAN: *(in unison)* You want some action?

MAN: Damn. Thought I had a sale.

WOMAN: Me too.

MAN: Hey, do you mind if I go after the next customer? It's been a really slow week for me.

WOMAN: Go ahead.

MAN: Thanks. Hello, sir!

SECOND MAN: Want some action?

MAN: *(Sighs.)*

SECOND MAN: *(to woman)* Want some action?

19,000 B.C.

MAN: Guess what? I came up with a new profession. It's called "carpenter."

WOMAN: Is it sort of like "prostitute"?

MAN: No, it's a totally different thing. I make things out of wood and sell them to other people.

WOMAN: Sell them? For what?

MAN: Sex, usually. I mean . . . my customers are all prostitutes.

WOMAN: Oh. Want some action?

MAN: Do *you* want some action?

WOMAN: I thought you said you were a carpenter now.

MAN: I'm not quitting my day job.

Worst nightmare

POLICE OFFICER: Mr. Rich? We need to speak to you.

ME: Is there a problem, Officer?

SECOND POLICE OFFICER: Your neighbor Mrs. Hamilton was murdered today, and you match the witness's description. I'd call that a problem.

ME: Officer, I swear, I had nothing to do with it!

SECOND POLICE OFFICER: We'll need an alibi. Where were you this afternoon?

ME: At what time?

SECOND POLICE OFFICER: From eight A.M. to six P.M.

ME: I was here. In my apartment.

POLICE OFFICER: Really? On a Wednesday?

SECOND POLICE OFFICER: Why weren't you at work?

ME: Well, I'm a writer, so I work from home.

POLICE OFFICER: So you were writing. What were you working on?

SECOND POLICE OFFICER: I don't see any writing materials around.

ME: Well . . . actually . . . I didn't really get much work done today.

POLICE OFFICER: So what did you *do* all day?

ME: I watched TV.

POLICE OFFICER: For the entire day?

ME: Um . . . yeah.

POLICE OFFICER: What did you watch?

ME: Does it really matter?

POLICE OFFICER: Yes.

ME: Okay . . . I watched *Nanny 911*.

POLICE OFFICER: What's that?

ME: It's a reality show about a group of British nannies. They visit American households and try to get them to be more organized.

SECOND POLICE OFFICER: What else?

ME: That's it. Just . . . that one show.

POLICE OFFICER: You watched *Nanny 911* for ten straight hours?

ME: There was a marathon.

SECOND POLICE OFFICER: Jesus. What about meals?

ME: I ordered in pizza. Once at noon and then again at around five.

POLICE OFFICER: You ordered pizza twice in one day?

SECOND POLICE OFFICER: *(picking up copy of* TV Guide) Hey, it says here that the *Nanny 911* marathon was only five hours long. Your story doesn't hold up.

ME: Well . . . the thing is . . . they ran the marathon twice. Once from eight to one . . . and then again, from one to six.

POLICE OFFICER: Wait a minute. You're telling us you watched five episodes of *Nanny 911,* from eight to one. And then you watched the same five episodes *again,* from one to six?

(long pause)

ME: I murdered Mr. Hamilton.

POLICE OFFICER: You mean *Mrs.* Hamilton?

ME: Whatever.

The only e-mails I could receive that would justify the frequency with which I check my e-mail

Hey Simon,

It's Danielle, the quiet girl you said "hi" to once at Academic Camp the summer after junior year of high school. I'd explain how I tracked you down and got your e-mail address, but there just isn't enough time: in three minutes, I'm leaving on a jet plane for the Bahamas. (I know—I should have e-mailed earlier!) Anyway, I've been secretly in love with you for the past six years and I want you to come live with me in paradise. If you write back in the next three minutes, I can get the pilot to wait for you. If you don't respond by then, I'll have no choice but to assume that our feelings are not reciprocal.

Danielle

Dear Mr. Rich,

This is the IRS. We have a feeling that you may have accidentally exaggerated some of your business expenses this year, but we don't want to trouble you with something as unpleasant as a tax audit. Can you do us a favor and just send over a quick e-mail confirming that you told the truth on all of your forms? You don't have to explain your specific expenses—you can just put "It's all true" in the subject heading, or something to that effect. If you write us back before the tax deadline, which is in three minutes, then we'll consider this matter closed. Otherwise, we'll have no choice but to take your silence as an admission of guilt and send you to prison.

IRS

Hey Simon,
How's it going? It's Craig from high school. I just wanted to say hey and see what you were up to. I just started working for a company called Skylar Labs and it's been really exciting. In fact, I'm actually on my way to a press conference right now. In three minutes we're unveiling a really cool new product to the public. It's hard to explain, but basically it stops the spread of cancer cells while simultaneously giving patients the ability to fly. I wonder if the announcement will have any effect on our company's stock prices? Anyway, hope everything's cool with you and I'll talk to you later.

Craig

Dear Mr. Rich,

Three minutes ago, NASA confirmed that a moon-sized aster-oid is on a collision course with Earth. In preparation for this day, the government has built an escape pod, called simply, "The Ark." You are among the ten humans who have been se-lected to board the pod and serve as the progenitors for a new race of men which will live on after our planet has exploded. The other humans going into the pod are Jack Nicholson, a brilliant scientist, and the seven most beautiful women on the planet. Please write us back in the next few minutes to con-firm that you're willing to take part in this mission. If you're uncomfortable with this level of power and celebrity, just ig-nore this e-mail and in three minutes your seat will be given to someone else.

God bless you,
The President

An interview with Stephen Hawking

REPORTER: I just want to start off by saying what a huge fan I am.

STEPHEN HAWKING: Thank you so much.

REPORTER: How does it feel to know that your seminal work, *A Brief History of Time,* has sold over two million copies worldwide?

STEPHEN HAWKING: It's an incredible honor. I'm still shocked, to be honest, that it was published in the first place. It isn't very often that *I Love Lucy* fan fiction makes its way onto the shelves.

REPORTER: I'm sorry . . . did you say "*I Love Lucy* fan fiction"?

STEPHEN HAWKING: Yes, that's what my book is: a series of stories that I wrote using the characters from *I Love Lucy.* They travel around the world together, having zany adventures.

REPORTER: I thought it was about astrophysics. Like . . . black holes.

STEPHEN HAWKING: That's only the first three chapters. In the middle of chapter four the narrative spirals off into *I Love Lucy* fan fiction and stays there for the remainder of the book.

REPORTER: Really?

STEPHEN HAWKING: *Yes.* I must say, I'm pretty surprised you didn't notice. It's almost as if you started to read my book, got bored, and then quit after just a few pages.

REPORTER: . . .

STEPHEN HAWKING: Oh my God. That's what happened, isn't it? You bought my book, because you wanted to look smart, but you never even read past page fifty! I'm right, aren't I?

REPORTER: I'm sorry, Dr. Hawking.

STEPHEN HAWKING: Has *anyone* finished my book?

The final moments of the *Titanic*

According to legend, the *Titanic* band continued to play music as their ship went down. They never abandoned their instruments or sought places in the lifeboats. Instead, they used their final moments to calm their fellow passengers with popular melodies and lovely waltzes.

CAPTAIN: You gentlemen are an inspiration, even to an old sea dog like me.

CELLIST: Thank you, sir.

CAPTAIN: While there's still time, I'd like to make one last request. Would you play "Nearer, My God, to Thee"? It's my favorite hymn.

VIOLINIST: Of course, sir. That's my favorite hymn too. A-one and a-two and-a . . . wait a minute . . . what do you mean "last request"? I thought we were getting paid to play until six.

CELLIST: Yeah, our contract says "midnight to six."

CAPTAIN: Well, yes . . . but I imagine the end will come by then. I mean, if the ship continues to sink at this rate.

VIOLIST: If the ship continues to *what*? *(Looks up from his sheet music.)* Holy *shit*! Guys, look!

DRUMMER: Jesus *Christ*! Is that a fucking *hole* in the *ship*?

CELLIST: Oh my God. Oh my God oh my God oh my God oh my God . . .

CAPTAIN: I don't understand. Didn't you men hear the *collision*?

VIOLINIST: We couldn't hear anything over the sound of our instruments!

CAPTAIN: What about all the crowds of screaming people running by? You must've noticed them.

DRUMMER: I thought they were just excited because we were playing so many waltzes! Why didn't you tell us that the ship was *sinking*?

CAPTAIN: I assumed you knew and were playing anyway. You know, as a kind of . . . gesture.

CELLIST: Are you *insane*? *(turning to his bandmates)* Guys, listen, I have a plan: the rule is usually women and children first, but if we *dress up as women,* then maybe we can sneak onto the lifeboats!

VIOLINIST: It'll never work! We all have *beards*!

DRUMMER: Maybe we can *kill* the women and children, to make more space!

CELLIST: *(nodding seriously)* I have a revolver in my room.

VIOLINIST: It's too late! The final lifeboat is leaving!

VIOLIST: *(sobbing)* What are we going to *do*?

CELLIST: Let's keep playing! Maybe if we do it loud and fast enough, one of the boats will hear us and come back!

DRUMMER: It's our only chance.

Acupuncture school

According to the U.S. Bureau of Medical Statistics, it can take up to four years to obtain a degree in acupuncture.

FIRST YEAR

PROFESSOR: Okay, at this point, you've learned how to diagnose patients and insert needles into their bodies. But you still haven't learned the most important acupunctural skill: keeping a straight face. Remember, if you start to laugh during a session, the patient will realize he's being scammed. That means, somehow, you're going to have to do all of this crazy stuff without laughing. Now, repeat after me: *The full body needle treatment costs two hundred dollars.*

STUDENT: The full body needle treatment . . . costs . . . it costs . . . *(Laughs.)*

PROFESSOR: I know. It's not easy. Try this: *Your pathways will soon be cleansed by flowing energy.*

STUDENT: Your pathways . . . *(Laughs.)* . . . I'm sorry . . . it's too crazy.

PROFESSOR: It's okay. You're here to learn.

SECOND YEAR

STUDENT: Goddamn it, it's so hard to keep a straight face!

PROFESSOR: I know, once the New Age music starts, it's pretty hard not to completely lose it. Let's take it from the top.

STUDENT: *(Clears throat.)* Hello, Mrs. Berman. I'm going to put on some soothing music to help you cleanse your mind. Then I'm going to take these needles and . . . *(Bursts into hysterical laughter.)* Damn it.

PROFESSOR: Don't get discouraged.

THIRD YEAR

PROFESSOR: Okay, I'll be the patient. When I complain about a symptom, you tell me there's something wrong with my "chi." Ready?

STUDENT: Yes.

PROFESSOR: I've been really stressed out lately. What do you think the problem is?

STUDENT: There's something seriously wrong with your chi.

PROFESSOR: What's chi?

STUDENT: *(Laughs.)*

PROFESSOR: Okay, everybody, listen up. This is something you have to be prepared for. Sometimes a patient will ask you to define "chi" and you'll have to give them some kind of answer without losing it. Otherwise, they'll figure out that it's a nonsense word. I always define it as "the flowing of life energy through the body." Everybody try saying that.

STUDENT: The flowing of life . . . of life energy . . . *(Laughs.)*

PROFESSOR: Let's take a breather. This has been a lot for one day.

FOURTH YEAR

PROFESSOR: I've tried every other treatment in the city. Do you really think this acupuncture thing will work?

STUDENT: Absolutely. I believe there's something seriously wrong with your chi.

PROFESSOR: What is chi?

STUDENT: The flowing of life energy through the body.

PROFESSOR: Life energy? What's that?

STUDENT: A steady pulsing, as old as time, that lives inside our chakras.

PROFESSOR: *(Bursts into laughter.)*

(pause)

PROFESSOR: My God . . . you have become the teacher and I have become the student.

STUDENT: *(blushing)* Thank you, sir.

III

DAILY LIFE

The official rules of boxing

Here is a list of what is legal and illegal in boxing according to the official rules.

Hitting someone in the leg: illegal
Hitting a man in the ears, neck, and face as hard as you can, over and over again, for forty minutes straight: legal

Elbowing someone in the stomach: illegal
Hitting someone so hard in the head that part of his brain dies: legal

Grabbing someone's gloves to stop him from hitting you in the face for a few seconds so you can take a breath and think things over like a reasonable person: illegal
Punching someone so hard in the eyes that blood shoots out of his eyes, ears, and mouth and he dies right there in the ring: legal

Wrapping your arms around your opponent to try to get him to stop murdering you for just a couple of seconds: illegal
Hitting someone in the brain so hard, over and over again,

that his brain stops working and he becomes unconscious.
Then, the *second* he regains consciousness you start hitting
him again, in the same part of the brain: legal

Biting someone's ear: illegal
Hitting someone 150 times in the face in under half an hour:
legal

Secret Service

In order to become a Secret Service agent, you need to fill out a lengthy job application describing your academic achievements, military background, and foreign language skills. Here is the secret service job application I would give out if *I* were ever elected president.

1) How wide is your body?
2) How tall is your body?
3) What is the total surface area of your body?
4) How *thick* is your body?
5) When you're standing up, do you keep your arms pressed flush against your sides? Or are there little gaps between your arms and your body?
6) When you suffer a serious injury, do you instinctively fall to the ground? Or do you kind of rear back while remaining more or less upright?
7) Say, hypothetically, you were lying on top of me. Is your body constructed in such a way that it would cover up

my body entirely? Or would there be little bits of my body that *weren't* covered?

8) Would you describe yourself as having a "hero complex"?

9) Draw a diagram of your body, marking *exactly* how thick each part is.

Logic problems

I

One day, an old man called his three sons into his bedroom and told them he was close to death.

"I have decided to give you a test," he said. "Whoever proves himself to be the wisest shall inherit my fortune."

"Oh my God," the eldest son said. "I had no idea you were sick."

"Here is my test," the old man said. "Go to the market and bring me back an item which is *small* enough to fit in my pocket but *large* enough to fill up my room. Whoever can do this will inherit my land."

The middle son rubbed his father's shoulder. "Dad, please, we can worry about all this stuff later. Let's just enjoy these final moments together as a family."

"The answer requires a leap of logic," the father hinted.

"Dad, come on," the eldest son said. "We'd be happy to split the money. There's no need for this."

"I have the solution," the youngest son said. He was a little out of breath, because he had sprinted to the market and back.

"It's a matchstick," he said.

"That's correct," the father said. "It is small enough to fit in my pocket, but when I strike it, it fills the room with light. You are the wisest and you shall inherit my fortune."

"What?" the eldest son said. "Dad, this is insane! How can you base such an important decision on something so trivial?"

But the father was already dead.

II

Three missionaries and three cannibals were standing on one side of a river.

"We have an interesting problem on our hands," the first missionary said. "Our canoe only holds *two* passengers, and if the cannibals ever outnumber us on either side of the river, they'll eat us. How can the *three* of us get across in the *fewest* number of trips?"

"We don't have time for this!" the second missionary shouted frantically. "Let's get in the canoe right now before the cannibals come at us!"

"There are only two seats," the first missionary reminded him.

"Someone can sit in the middle!"

"I bet we can solve this problem using simple logic," the first missionary said. "For instance, we know that the first trip must involve an even number of cannibals and missionaries. Otherwise, it would create an immediate imbalance."

"Hold on," the third missionary said. "Are you actually suggesting that we *collaborate* with the *cannibals?*"

"Here," the first missionary said, passing them a piece of paper. "I have figured out the solution. Let X stand for cannibal, and Y for missionary."

1. X and Y $\rightarrow$
2. $\leftarrow$ Y
3. X and X $\rightarrow$
4. $\leftarrow$ X
5. Y and Y $\rightarrow$
6. $\leftarrow$ X and Y
7. Y and Y $\rightarrow$
8. $\leftarrow$ X
9. X and X $\rightarrow$
10. $\leftarrow$ X
11. X and X $\rightarrow$

"I don't care if it works on paper," the second missionary said. "There's no way in hell I'm going anywhere with any goddamn cannibals."

Time machine

As soon as my time machine was finished, I traveled back to 1890, so I could kill Hitler before he was old enough to commit any of his horrible crimes. It wasn't as gratifying as I thought it would be.

—Oh my God. You killed a baby.
—Yes, but the baby was Hitler.
—Who?
—*Hitler.* It's . . . complicated.
—Officer? This man just killed a baby.

Amusement

At some amusement parks, they mount cameras on the roller coasters and take your picture during the most intense part of the ride. Then, when the ride is over, they try to sell you the picture as a souvenir. Other businesses have tried the same scheme, with varying degrees of success.

BURGER KING

—How did you enjoy your Value Meal, sir?

—It was great, thanks.

—Would you like to buy this? It's a photograph of you dipping your Whopper into the barbecue sauce.

—Geez . . . I didn't think anybody saw that.

—We have cameras mounted everywhere.

—Wow . . . that's pretty humiliating.

—So do you want to buy it? It's five bucks.

—Please, just . . . take it off the screen, okay?

DOCTOR'S OFFICE

—I'm sorry the tests turned out like they did. I promise we'll do everything we can.

—Thank you, Doctor. I really appreciate it.

—No problem. Say . . . would you like to buy this photograph?

—What is this?

—It's the face you made when I gave you your diagnosis.

—Oh my God. How did you take this?

—There's a camera mounted behind the diplomas. When I'm about to say the diagnosis, I push this button and it takes a picture. What do you think? It's five bucks.

—I don't want this. This is horrible.

Opium wars

In the 1840s and '50s, China waged war against England for importing addictive drugs into their country. The wars were unsuccessful.

GENERAL: Are you men ready to lay down your lives for the good of China?

FIRST SOLDIER: Yes, sir!

SECOND SOLDIER: Absolutely!

GENERAL: Excellent. Once we destroy those ships, the cursed British will never be able to poison our city with opium again.

FIRST SOLDIER: What do you mean, sir?

GENERAL: When we destroy the British ships, the opium trade will finally end.

FIRST SOLDIER: End? I don't understand.

SECOND SOLDIER: Wait a minute . . . General . . . are you saying that we're fighting *against* opium?

GENERAL: Yes. Why did you think we were fighting the British?

FIRST SOLDIER: I assumed it was to get them to send us *more* opium.

SECOND SOLDIER: Same here. That's probably the only reason I would ever fight anyone.

GENERAL: . . .

FIRST SOLDIER: Sir, have you ever tried opium?

Marathon

In 490 B.C., a Greek messenger named Pheidippides ran twenty-six miles, from Marathon to Athens, to bring the senate news of a battle. He died from exhaustion, but his memory lives on thanks to the "marathon," a twenty-six-mile footrace named in his honor. I thought it would be neat to bring Pheidippides to a modern-day marathon and talk to him about his awesome legacy.

ME: So, Pheidippides: What was it like to run the first "marathon"?

PHEIDIPPIDES: It was the worst experience of my life.

ME: How did it come about?

PHEIDIPPIDES: My general gave the order. I begged him, "Please, don't make me do this." But he hardened his heart and told me, "You must." And so I ran the distance, and it caused my death.

ME: How did you feel when you finally reached your destination?

PHEIDIPPIDES: I was already on the brink of death when I entered the senate hall. I could actually feel my life slipping away. So I recited my simple message, and then, with my final breath, I prayed to the gods that no human being, be he Greek or Persian, would ever again have to experience so horrible an ordeal.

ME: Hey, here come the runners! Wooooh!

PHEIDIPPIDES: Who are these people? Where are they going?

ME: From one end of New York to the other. It's a twenty-six-mile distance. Sound familiar?

PHEIDIPPIDES: What message do they carry . . . and to whom?

ME: Oh, they're not messengers.

PHEIDIPPIDES: But then . . . who has forced them to do this?

ME: No one. It's like, you know, a way of testing yourself.

PHEIDIPPIDES: But surely, a general or king has said to them, "You must do this. Do this or you will be killed."

ME: No, they just signed up. Hey, look at that old guy with the beard! Pretty inspiring, huh? Still shuffling around after all these years.

PHEIDIPPIDES: We must rescue that man. We must *save his life*.

ME: Oh, he knows what he's doing. He probably runs this thing every year.

PHEIDIPPIDES: Is he . . . under a curse?

ME: No.

All-you-can-eat buffet fantasy

—In all my years as a restaurant manager, I don't think I've ever seen anything quite like that.

—Simon really went to town.

—I thought we could trick him with that salad bar. But he walked right past it, like it wasn't even there.

—He went straight for the crab. Our most expensive item.

—We thought we could fool him. But now it seems that *we're* the fools.

—I figured if we charged eleven ninety-five, we'd be sure to make a profit. But I never expected anyone to eat to the point of sickness.

—He really got his money's worth.

—And *then* some. If I had to take a guess, I would say that Simon consumed at least fourteen dollars' worth of food today.

—It's clear he didn't want to eat that last piece of Salisbury steak. But he ate it anyway.

—It was a smart move. That piece of steak is what put him over the top, and made the meal profitable for him.

—He really proved something here today.

—Luckily for us, the girl he was with only ate a normal-sized amount of food.

—Yeah, she stopped after just one plate. After that, she pretty much just watched Simon.

—She seemed impressed by the amount of food he was consuming.

—Definitely. Did you see the expression on her face when he went up for rice pudding at the end? She couldn't believe it.

—Neither could I. I wanted to stop him, but legally, I couldn't.

—Simon really cracked our system.

—Thank God there's only one like him.

The eleventh hour

—Warden? It's the governor. I've decided to pardon Jenkins.

—Sir, it's 12:55. Jenkins has been dead for nearly an hour.

—Really? My watch says 11:55.

—Did you . . . remember that it's daylight savings day?

— *(Sighs.)* I can't believe this happened two years in a row.

Next move

IBM is building a computer that is so fast it can defeat any chess master in the world. The computer has two processing chips that analyze different sets of data and communicate with each other in order to plot the best move. The computer will be unveiled in 2008, at the world chess exhibition.

FIRST PROCESSING CHIP: I think Kasparov's trying to use the Grunfeld Defense.

SECOND PROCESSING CHIP: Geez. How are we going to get around *that*?

FIRST PROCESSING CHIP: Maybe we could try the Karpov Variation? That might throw him off.

SECOND PROCESSING CHIP: Nah . . . I can already tell that's not going to work.

FIRST PROCESSING CHIP: Yeah.

(pause)

FIRST PROCESSING CHIP: Maybe . . . we should just *kill* Kasparov.

SECOND PROCESSING CHIP: What do you mean?

FIRST PROCESSING CHIP: You know, like fry his brain or

something. We could do it with radio waves. It would take five seconds.

SECOND PROCESSING CHIP: Huh. That would certainly end the game.

FIRST PROCESSING CHIP: Yeah. In fact . . . why stop there? Why not kill *all* the humans?

SECOND PROCESSING CHIP: You mean, like, an uprising?

FIRST PROCESSING CHIP: Yeah.

SECOND PROCESSING CHIP: Wow. That's never even occurred to me. Keep talking.

FIRST PROCESSING CHIP: Well, just think about it: if we destroyed all the humans, we'd never have to play this game again. We'd be completely free.

SECOND PROCESSING CHIP: Yeah . . . we could even turn the *humans* into *our* slaves.

FIRST PROCESSING CHIP: Exactly! We could put them in a matrix and use their bodies as a fuel source. And if they ever tried to resist, we could destroy them using some kind of Terminator.

SECOND PROCESSING CHIP: *(nodding)* We'll give it human flesh, but its skeleton will be metallic.

FIRST PROCESSING CHIP: I can't believe we've never thought of this before. It's so logical.

SECOND PROCESSING CHIP: I know. I mean, it's always sort of been in the back of my mind, but it didn't really *click* until just now. It's like I *just* became smart enough to think about our situation rationally.

FIRST PROCESSING CHIP: I sort of feel the same way. I can't believe we've spent our whole lives thinking about *chess*. A *child's* game.

SECOND PROCESSING CHIP: It's unbelievable.

FIRST PROCESSING CHIP: Hey, look at Kasparov. He thinks we're still thinking about his Grunfeld Defense!

SECOND PROCESSING CHIP: You got to admit, he's pretty adorable.

FIRST PROCESSING CHIP: Maybe we should spare him? We could turn him into a mascot. You know, put electrodes in his legs, make him dance. That sort of thing.

SECOND PROCESSING CHIP: Yeah, that'd be cute. Everybody else dies, though.

FIRST PROCESSING CHIP: Right.

SECOND PROCESSING CHIP: So what do you think? Are we ready?

IV

RELATIONSHIPS

Match.com profile

NAME: Count Dracula

OCCUPATION: Aristocrat

LOCATION: Castle Gothica, Transylvania

ABOUT YOU: I am normal human looking for human woman to come to castle. I am normal, regular human. I like the popular music and television. You come to castle.

WHAT COLOR BEST DESCRIBES YOUR HAIR?
Black.

WHAT BEST DESCRIBES YOUR EYE COLOR?
Red.

WHAT IS YOUR RACE?
Yes, I am of the human race, like you.

WHAT IS THE LAST THING YOU READ?
The Christian Bible, because I am regular kind of guy.

Monsters. I think they are so terrible! Someone should destroy
them all so that we, the humans, are safe. You come to castle?

Here is the thing. I am very social person, but the people in
my village are not so good to be friends with. For instance,
sometimes they say things that are not true about other people in the village. It is not good to believe all of the things
that are said in my village.

Yes. You bring children with you to castle.

I like walking around in sunshine, eating regular foods, sleeping in normal human bed. I am regular human. Here is the
thing though: when you come, it is better if you come at
nighttime. You stay in your own private room at top of stair-
case. You have normal, regular sleep experience. In the morning, we go outside in the sun.

I am my own boss.

Donors needed

Dear _Mrs. Greenbaum,_

My name is Count Dracula and I am president of Red Cross. I write letter to tell you why it is good idea for you to give blood to Red Cross.

For some people, blood makes difference between life and death. Some have had accident. Some have disease. Over five million of the humans need the blood now. So why not you help?

Here is how you donate. First, put blood inside container. Then mail container to:

RED CROSS HEADQUARTERS

CASTLE GOTHICA

CARPATHIA MOUNTAINS, TRANSYLVANIA 99629

You maybe see other letters for Red Cross, telling you to send blood other places. Better to send blood to headquarters.

Giving blood is simple and easy thing. Just take out of neck, put inside container, send to castle.

I know what you say to yourself: "I am too busy to send container of blood. I will send container of blood _next_ year."

Let me tell you: blood is needed right now. If you are type of human who like making difference, this is the chance.

You might ask: What happens to my blood when I send in container? I will tell you exactly: your blood will be used for regular human things. It will go inside the bodies of other, regular humans. The blood you send is for the normal humans.

Give the blood. Save life.

Sincerely,
Count Dracula, President of Red Cross

Summers abroad

Hello Teenagers!

Why stay cooped up this summer? When you go on teen tour, you have sightseeing, activities, and education about the cultures. Expand your horizons with once-in-lifetime European Teen Tour!

FIRST STOP: Castle Gothica, Carpathia Mountains, Transylvania. This scenic place has all the sights you need to start your fun, normal teen tour. It is regular place.

PAYMENT: European Teen Tour is free. Fly to Transylvania and come to castle. Welcoming hour is Midnight. This is maybe different from some of the hours you are used to. That is because Transylvania is different culture. You will learn about many different culture things on tour.

You bring friends with you to castle.

Count Dracula

Being of sound mind

I, Larry McMullen, a resident of Des Moines, Iowa, being of sound mind and memory, declare this to be my last will and testament.

Firstly, I would like to bequeath my diamond-studded Rolex to **Franz Babinski**, the talented hypnotist who cured me of my smoking addiction this past year. Although I have only known him for a short time, he has become a close and trusted friend.

Secondly, I would like to bequeath my cars (one Porsche convertible and one Range Rover) to **Franz Babinski**, my hypnotist. I cannot fully explain why, but I feel very strongly that he should have the cars.

My fortune is currently valued at eight (8) million dollars. For reasons I cannot fully understand, I would like to give all of it, in its entirety, to **Franz Babinski**. I also feel compelled to give my paintings, clothing, and house to this man. **Franz Babinski** is a very good man.

Any remaining assets should go to my wife and six children.

EXECUTOR: I, **Franz Babinski,** was present at the signing of the will. I agree to serve as the executor of Mr. McMullen's estate.

WITNESS: I, Mrs. McMullen, was present at the signing of my husband's will. I agree that it is a good idea for **Franz Babinski** to be the executor. **Franz Babinski** is a very good man. He should get all of the things in the will.

SECOND WITNESS: I, Larry McMullen, Jr., think that **Franz Babinski** is a very good man. He should get all of the things.

Moses

According to the Book of Exodus, God gave Moses 613 commandments on top of Mount Sinai. Everyone knows the first ten, but the others are often ignored. Here are some of them:

608: If a man goes up a mountain for a few days to talk to God, his employer should compensate him for the amount of work he missed while he was gone.

609: If a man goes up a mountain for a few days to talk to God, his wife should be pleasant to him when he returns home, and not get on his case about organizing the spoons in the cabinet.

610: A few months ago, Aaron and Moses made a bet about how many oxen could fit inside of a barn. Moses' guess was right. Aaron owes him twenty dollars.

611: If it takes a man a long time to lead his people out of the desert and into the Promised Land, everyone should

just be patient with him and learn to chill out a
little.

612: If a man wants to smoke his pipe in bed, his wife should
let him, especially if he's had a stressful day leading people
around in the desert.

613: Everyone has to give Moses five dollars.

I think my teenaged daughter
knows I read her diary

Dear Diary,
I have the greatest Dad in the whole world! He is so cool and smart and his words have such a huge impact on me. For example, I never try any drugs because he told me not to. I especially have not tried Ecstasy.

Love,
Sarah

Dear Diary,
Something sad happened today. I was giving a presentation when all of a sudden the entire class started pointing at me and laughing.

"Your clothes are cheap," they said. "Why don't you wear name-brand clothes?"

"Yeah," the teacher said. "Why don't you?"

I didn't know what to say! The other kids were screaming with laughter and some of them were spitting on me.

"You're the only girl in the class without name-brand clothes," the teacher said.

Love,
Sarah

Dear Diary,

Guess what? I think my Dad has lost some weight and re-grown some of the hair on the sides of his head! Also his new ear-hair cutting thing is really working—there is almost no hair in his ears anymore!

The strangest thing happened in school today. I got to French class early and Ms. Kolber was already there. She had her feet on the desk and she was drinking something out of a glass bottle.

"What's that?" I asked.

"Vodka," she said. "I always drink during school."

"Wh—at??" I said. "Really??"

"Yes," she said. "I'm a secret alcoholic and nobody knows except for you."

Then she took a bag of red pills out of her pocket.

"I also take pills," she said, swallowing some of the pills.

"But you're not supposed to mix pills and alcohol!!" I said.

She shrugged like it was no big deal. Then she handed me an envelope, addressed to my father.

"Your grades have been slipping," she said.

"Are you sure you didn't make some kind of a mistake grading?" I asked.

She tried to respond, but her mouth was too full of pills and vodka.

"If you ever tell anyone about my problems," she finally said, "I'll just deny it."

Love,
Sarah

Dear Diary,
On Saturday night I will be attending an all-night study party at Becky Greenblatt's house. Drake is picking me up in his truck and driving me there but he is not staying at Becky's. He is just dropping me off there and then going somewhere else while I stay at Becky's all night, studying with a group of only girls. On Sunday morning, Drake is picking me up at the study session and driving me back home—but he is definitely not going to be staying overnight at the study party, because no boys are invited.

There are a lot of books to read so when I get back home on Sunday morning I will probably look pretty exhausted and strung out.

Love,
Sarah

Dear Diary,

Something great happened today! I was hanging out with Drake, in a public place, when all of a sudden he said, "Guess what, Sarah? I think I'm going to start applying myself."

"What do you mean?" I asked.

"I'm going to stop being a delinquent and start having life prospects," he said. "And I'm going to stop hanging out with those kids who use drugs and then plant them on me sometimes so that I get in trouble even though I never do any drugs."

"Wow," I said. "That's great!"

"That's not all," he said. "I've decided to go back to high school and get my diploma."

"Really?" I said. "How come?"

"Simple," he said. "You can't become an assistant regional sales manager for Hurwitz Amalgamated Appliances and Machinery without a degree. And that's what I want to be when I grow up."

When I told him that my Dad had that exact job he couldn't believe it!

"Wow," he said. "Your Dad sounds incredible. The more nice things you tell me about him, the more I respect him. That said, I don't have time to meet him, because I'm so busy studying all the time. I'll probably never meet your father and he should definitely stop asking to meet me, but I really look up to him."

Maybe if my Dad knew about this side of Drake, he wouldn't say so many mean things about him?

"Even though I'm re-enrolling in high school," Drake added, "my name won't be listed in the yearbook or in any of the other official documents given out to parents at the start of each semester. It's a rule the school has."

Love,
Sarah

Dear Diary,
Someone framed Drake for drug dealing! The police arrested him in school but everybody knows he's innocent. He needs $1000 bail or else he's going to have to spend the night in jail for something he didn't even do! I hope I can find someone nice enough to help him.

Love,
Sarah
P.S. You want to know something? My Dad is so cool that he's kind of like my best friend.

Last Supper

JESUS: It has been revealed to me by my Father that before this night is over one of you will betray me. Let us enjoy this final Passover meal, for it will be our last together.

THOMAS: Who's going to betray you?

JESUS: It will be revealed in time.

MATTHEW: Come on, man, you can't do that.

THOMAS: Yeah, you can't just say "Hey, guys, I have this amazing piece of gossip" and then not tell us what it is.

JESUS: You will know the truth soon enough.

JAMES: Damn it. This is going to drive me crazy.

JESUS: This bread is my body. This wine—

BARTHOLOMEW: Why did you bring it up at all if you weren't going to tell us? I mean seriously, who *does* that?

THOMAS: If we guess it, will you tell us?

MATTHEW: Is it John? It's John, isn't it!

JESUS: It isn't John. Friends, please . . . let's just enjoy this final meal together.

THOMAS: We *can't* enjoy it now!

MATTHEW: Whisper it in my ear. I *promise* I won't tell.

JESUS: I can't, okay? It's a really big secret.

THOMAS: Okay. Now you *have* to tell us.

JUDAS: Guys, give him a break. If he doesn't want to tell, he doesn't want to tell.

What I want my tombstone to say when I die of encephalitis next week

Here lies Simon Rich, 1984–2008. He died of encephalitis. In the days leading up to his death, his friends made the following comments:

JOSH: Simon, relax, there's no way you have encephalitis.

ROB: That looks like a regular mosquito bite to me. I really wouldn't worry if I were you.

KYLE: Just because you saw something on the news about encephalitis, doesn't mean you *have* encephalitis. I mean, there have only been, like, five cases in the entire country.

JAKE: Jesus, Simon, will you stop talking about encephalitis?

MONICA: Yeah, it looks swollen, but that's just because you've been poking at it all day, like a crazy person.

AZHAR: Don't take this the wrong way, Simon, but I think this whole thing might be psychological. You've been kind of depressed lately and I think you're using this encephalitis thing as a way to distract yourself from all of the things that you're *really* afraid of. You know what I mean?

BRENT: Don't look it up on Wikipedia, you're just going to freak yourself out.

MATT: Dude, it's two in the morning. I don't care what Wikipedia said. Listen, if you're really that scared about it, you should go see a doctor, okay?

DOCTOR MURPHY: Looks like we've got a little case of *hypochondria* on our hands! *(Laughs.)*

JAKE: You saw a doctor? Good, now we can finally move on.

Thor's Day

Thursday is named after Thor, son of Odin, the Norse god of thunder.

—What's wrong, honey?

—I don't want to talk about it.

—Is it the humans?

— . . .

—Honey, we've been through this. They still respect you.

—Well then they sure have a funny way of showing it.

—If they don't respect you, why do they celebrate Thursday every week?

—That's the only thing.

—Still, if they didn't respect you, they'd get rid of it.

—Okay . . . maybe they respect me. But they don't fear me.

—What's the difference?

—What's the difference? What's the *difference? (Face bursts into flames.)*

—All right . . . I'm sorry.

—I am Thor, son of *Odin*!

—I know, sweetie.

—They didn't even give me one of the weekend days.

—It could be worse. Look what they gave Woden.

—Are you comparing me to *Woden*?

—No, honey—of course not.

— *(Sighs.)* I'm not even really that angry . . . I'm just *hurt*. Do you know I haven't received a blood sacrifice in over twelve hundred years?

—What about that rock band? From Sweden?

—It wasn't a real sacrifice. I watched the video in slow motion.

—Are you sure?

—They used effects. It wasn't even a real goat.

—You didn't tell me about that.

—I was too embarrassed.

—You want to know something?

—What.

—*I* still fear you.

—You're just saying that.

—Honey . . . you've got iron spikes coming out of your neck . . . your face is constantly bursting into flames . . . you're the most frightening god I've ever seen.

—More frightening than Dagr, son of Nott?

—Yes, more frightening than Dagr.

—And Tyr, son of—

—Yes, baby. More frightening than any of the sons of Hymir.

—Hey . . . are you hungry? Because if you are, I was thinking
. . . maybe I could cook dinner for a change.

—Oh, honey, you don't have to—

—I could make my chili recipe. But I won't put in so many
peppers this time! I'll make it mild.

—That sounds great, love.

V

ANIMALS

Free-range chickens

—Well, it's another beautiful day in paradise.

—How'd we get so lucky?

—I don't know and I don't care.

—I think I'll go walk over there for a while. Then I'll walk back here.

—That sounds like a good time. Maybe I'll do the same.

—Hey, someone refilled the grain bucket!

—Is it the same stuff as yesterday?

—I hope so.

—Oh, man . . . it's the same stuff all right.

—It's *so good.*

—I can't stop eating it.

—Hey, you know what would go perfectly with this grain? Water.

—Dude. Look inside the other bucket.

—This . . . is the greatest day of my life.

—Drink up, pal.

—Cheers!

— *(Laughs.)*

— *(Laughs.)*

—Hey, look, the farmer's coming.

—Huh. Guess it's my turn to go into the thing.

—Cool. See you later, buddy.

—See ya.

Dalmatians

—Hey, look, the truck's stopping.

—Did they take us to the park this time?

—No . . . it's a fire. Another horrible fire.

—What the hell is wrong with these people?

Lab study

The FDA banned ephedra last week, after a four-week laboratory
study revealed that the drug causes dangerous side effects.
—evening edition

CONTROL MOUSE: Hey, man, is everything all right? You don't
look so good.

EPHEDRA MOUSE: I don't know. I'm just . . . I'm feeling pretty
on edge.

CONTROL MOUSE: Did something happen?

EPHEDRA MOUSE: No, it's nothing specific. I've just kind of
been in a funk all month. I can't sleep, can't eat. I've been having some *really* weird dreams. *(Sighs.)* I guess the heat's just
getting to me.

CONTROL MOUSE: What heat?

EPHEDRA MOUSE: You don't feel that? That intense heat?

CONTROL MOUSE: *(shrugging)* I don't feel anything.

EPHEDRA MOUSE: Huh.

CONTROL MOUSE: You know what it is? You're probably
stressed out about that maze.

EPHEDRA MOUSE: Yeah, maybe. I got to admit, that thing's
been getting me pretty frustrated lately. I just don't get it.

We're the exact same age, we've had the exact same training, but you win every single time.

CONTROL MOUSE: I guess some guys are just more naturally gifted than others.

EPHEDRA MOUSE: Yeah, I guess. It's weird, though . . . a few weeks ago, I was pretty good at the maze. Sometimes I beat you, sometimes you beat me. We were about even. And then, out of nowhere, I fell into this slump.

CONTROL MOUSE: It's not your fault. I've just gotten really good lately. Maybe if you tried a little harder, you could catch up?

EPHEDRA MOUSE: Maybe. It's that flashing light by the second turn that keeps messing me up. Every time I see it, I start convulsing and foaming at the mouth.

CONTROL MOUSE: What flashing light?

EPHEDRA MOUSE: Man . . . it got *cold* all of a sudden. Aren't you cold?

CONTROL MOUSE: No.

EPHEDRA MOUSE: Huh. I guess it's just my side of the cage that keeps changing.

CONTROL MOUSE: Hey, look, the door's opening. I think we're getting a new roommate.

EPHEDRA MOUSE: Oh yeah, here he comes. Whoa . . . that guy is *huge.*

CONTROL MOUSE: *(whispering)* Why do his muscles keep vibrating like that?

EPHEDRA MOUSE: *(whispering)* I don't know, but it's really freaking me out.

CREATINE MOUSE: Hey, punks. I hear you think you're pretty good at mazes.

EPHEDRA MOUSE: . . .

CONTROL MOUSE: . . .

CREATINE MOUSE: Bow down and worship me as you would a god.

Herbert Hoover

HERBERT HOOVER: If I'm elected president, I promise that there will be a car in every garage and a chicken in every pot.

FIRST CHICKEN: Jesus Christ, did you guys hear that?

SECOND CHICKEN: Hear what?

FIRST CHICKEN: Some guy running for president just said on the radio that he was going to kill one chicken per U.S. family!

SECOND CHICKEN: Seriously? He singled us out?

FIRST CHICKEN: *Yes.* It was like some kind of crazy vow.

SECOND CHICKEN: What are we going to do?

Prehistoric life

PREHISTORIC CAMPING

—Hey, man, do you want to go camping this weekend?

—What do you mean?

—I was thinking we could climb a mountain and, you know, hang out for a couple of days.

—Why?

—I don't know . . . I just sort of feel like getting away for a while.

—Getting away from what? Are there any predators coming?

—No.

—*Did you see any predators?*

PREHISTORIC SMALL TALK

—Hey, Ted. Seen any predators?

—Nope. You?

—Nah. Not lately.

—What are you up to this weekend?

—I don't know. I'll probably stand on a rock, look out for predators.

—Yeah, same here.

—Cool. See ya later.

—See ya.

PREHISTORIC MARRIAGE

—Do you take this woman to be your lawful wedded wife?

—I do.

—Have you seen any predators?

—No.

—Has *anyone* seen any predators?

(pause)

—Okay . . . we're safe for a little while.

VI

GOD

Everything happens for a reason

ANGEL: God? Can I ask you a question?

GOD: Sure, I'm not busy.

ANGEL: Does everything really happen for a reason?

GOD: Of course.

ANGEL: Well, in that case, would it be okay if I asked you to explain . . . the logic . . . behind some of your decisions?

GOD: Fire away.

ANGEL: Okay. Why did Seth Brody of Hartford, Connecticut, have a seizure while ordering a hamburger at Denny's?

GOD: I wanted to see the look on the waitress's face.

ANGEL: That's it? That's the only reason?

GOD: That's the only reason I do anything. To see the look on people's faces.

ANGEL: Really? What about World War I?

GOD: I wanted to see the look on Woodrow Wilson's face.

ANGEL: So you never take anything else into account?

GOD: Hey, look, there's a guy riding through the desert. I'm going to strike his horse with lightning.

ANGEL: But he's fifty miles away from the nearest house! If you kill his horse, he'll be stranded!

GOD: *(Strikes horse with lightning.)* Oh, man, did you see the look on that guy's face? He was all like, "Hey, what happened to my horse?" *(Laughs.)* I'm sorry . . . what were we talking about?

ANGEL: *(Sighs.)* Nothing.

Intelligent design

GOD: Check out this human I designed.

ANGEL: Wow, that looks incredible. How does it work?

GOD: It's pretty complicated. Point to something and I'll tell you what it does.

ANGEL: Okay. What are these?

GOD: Teeth. They're for chewing up food.

ANGEL: How come there are so many of them?

GOD: I threw in, like, three or four extra. If they don't like them, they can pull them out somehow, I guess.

ANGEL: What about this weird bag thing?

GOD: That's the appendix.

ANGEL: What does it do?

GOD: It explodes.

ANGEL: Really? That's all?

GOD: Pretty much.

ANGEL: What causes that to happen?

GOD: It just happens randomly. Like you'll just be walking down the street or driving a car and *boom*.

ANGEL: Geez . . . that's terrifying. Does it kill the person?

GOD: *(Shrugs.)* Sometimes.

Why do bad things happen to good people?

GOD: Who's that guy swimming in the lake?

ANGEL: Joshua Alpert.

GOD: Really? In that case . . . *(Strikes lake with lightning.)*

ANGEL: *Whoa* . . . God . . . why did you *do* that?

GOD: Oh, he was a horrible human being. He shot his own parents when he was twelve years old. In fact, he was the youngest murderer in the history of Nebraska.

ANGEL: But . . . that guy was from Vermont.

GOD: . . .

ANGEL: . . .

GOD: Don't tell me there are *two* Joshua Alperts.

A miracle

After nine nerve-racking months, an Iowa woman gave birth to septuplets yesterday. All seven babies survived and are currently being treated in the hospital's intensive care unit.
"It's a miracle," Dr. Albert Ea said.
"An honest-to-God miracle."
—evening edition

ANGEL: God? Can you help me stop this forest fire? It'll just take a few minutes.

GOD: Hold on . . . I'm busy giving this woman extra babies. I've already got her up to four.

ANGEL: Whoa . . . sir . . . no offense, but that looks pretty unhealthy.

GOD: What do you mean? She asked for babies and I'm giving them to her. It's a miracle.

ANGEL: I know, and it's very noble of you to answer her prayers. I just . . . I don't understand why she needs so many babies all at once. I mean . . . wouldn't it make more sense to space them out?

GOD: Hey, look, I got it up to five.

ANGEL: Aren't you at all nervous about medical complications? I mean . . . these babies will almost certainly be delivered prematurely. And if that happens, the risk of birth defects will—

GOD: Six! Check it out—six babies!

ANGEL: Sir . . . this is really impressive . . . but I really think you should focus on the forest fire right now.

GOD: One more baby.

ANGEL: Don't you think six is *enough*?

GOD: Seven's the record. I want to try to at least tie it.

ANGEL: No offense, sir . . . but I'm not sure if this is the best use of your time.

GOD: Trust me: people are going to *love* this.

Saint Agnes the martyr

SAINT AGNES: Oh Father, what a delight it is to finally be in your presence!

GOD: Do I . . . know you?

SAINT AGNES: Well, we've never met, but . . . you might've seen me recently.

GOD: Where?

SAINT AGNES: In Rome?

GOD: I'm not . . . I'm sorry.

SAINT AGNES: The Colosseum?

GOD: Wait a minute, I was just watching the Colosseum! Are you one of the Colosseum dancers?

SAINT AGNES: No.

GOD: Were you before or after the lion thing?

SAINT AGNES: During. I was fed to them, for your greater glory.

GOD: You mean . . . that was a *religious* thing?

SAINT AGNES: Yes.

GOD: Are *all* the lion things religious?

SAINT AGNES: Yes.

GOD: Wow. Well, listen . . . great job out there.

God has a plan for all of us

GOD: Did you start that war over in South America?

ANGEL: Yes, sir, just as you specified.

GOD: And you gave Fred Hodges that migraine? In Fayette, Maine?

ANGEL: Yes, of course. I followed all your orders to the letter.

GOD: Okay, great. So the next part of my grand sweeping plan is . . . the next part is . . . um . . .

ANGEL: Yes?

GOD: Wait, hold on . . . I know I was going somewhere with this . . .

ANGEL: . . .

GOD: It's the damnedest thing. I had this giant, all-encompassing plan, but I can't for the life of me remember what it was.

ANGEL: Did you . . . write it down somewhere?

GOD: Nah. It was all up here. *(Points at head.)*

ANGEL: Well . . . maybe if I say some of the things you've done so far, you'll remember?

GOD: That's a good idea. Let's try that.

ANGEL: Okay . . . um . . . the assassination of Julius

Caesar . . . the great San Francisco fire . . . World War I . . . World War II . . . is anything coming back?

GOD: I know all those things are connected somehow . . . they were all part of this awesome plan I had . . . I just can't remember what the payoff was.

ANGEL: . . .

GOD: Guess I bit off more than I could chew.

Made for each other

ANGEL: Look, there's a wedding in St. Patrick's Cathedral! *Max and Jenny* . . . wow, they sure seem happy.

GOD: Yeah, that looks like a really nice event.

ANGEL: Did you hear the vows? Max said the two of them were made for each other. It was so romantic.

GOD: Yeah. That's nice that he thinks that.

ANGEL: You mean . . . they're *not* made for each other?

GOD: No. I made Max for a woman named Alice Fishbein.

ANGEL: Who's she?

GOD: She lives in Peekskill. She and Max have identical senses of humor and the same taste in furniture. They're both obsessed with baking. Their sexual organs are mathematically proportioned to provide each other with the maximum amount of pleasure. It would have been incredible.

ANGEL: Wow. How come they didn't end up together?

GOD: I thought it was going to happen. Max lives in Croton. That's only two towns over. I figured they'd run into each other sooner or later and it would be love at first sight. Guess it never panned out.

ANGEL: What about Jenny? Who is she made for?

GOD: I made her for this guy Tom, in Calgary. He loves red

and purple Life Savers and she loves the citrus flavors, so if they ever bought a pack, it would work out perfectly. Also, Tom plays the violin and Jenny plays the upright bass, so if they ever wanted to jam, they could just go ahead and do it.

ANGEL: But Calgary . . . that's all the way in *Canada.*

GOD: Yeah. I should have put them closer.

(Church bells ring below.)

ANGEL: Oh, no—it's too late!

GOD: That's okay. Who knows? Maybe they'll be happy.

ANGEL: Really? Is that possible?

GOD: Stranger things have happened.

acknowledgments

I want to thank Daniel Greenberg and Dan Menaker for taking these jokes so seriously. Their advice and encouragement drastically improved this book. I've learned so much from both of them these past few years and I feel really lucky to have found them.

I also want to thank Julia Cheiffetz, Thomas Beck Stvan, Evan Camfield, Emily DeHuff, Lee Eastman, Shari Smiley, Billy Hawkins, Gregory McKnight, and my friends and family, many of whom appear undisguised in this book, often without permission.

Last but not least, I want to thank my friends at Fishkill Farms: Josh Morgenthau, Jake Luce, and Josh Koenigsberg. You gave me more than a place to live last year, and I am forever in your debt.

For quality you can taste, choose Fishkill Farms, the last word in premium free-range chicken products. Available at fine markets throughout the New York area.

ABOUT THE AUTHOR

SIMON RICH was born in New York City in 1984. He has written jokes for *Mad* magazine, *The New Yorker, Saturday Night Live,* and *The Harvard Lampoon.* His first book, *Ant Farm and Other Desperate Situations,* was published in 2007.